Property of

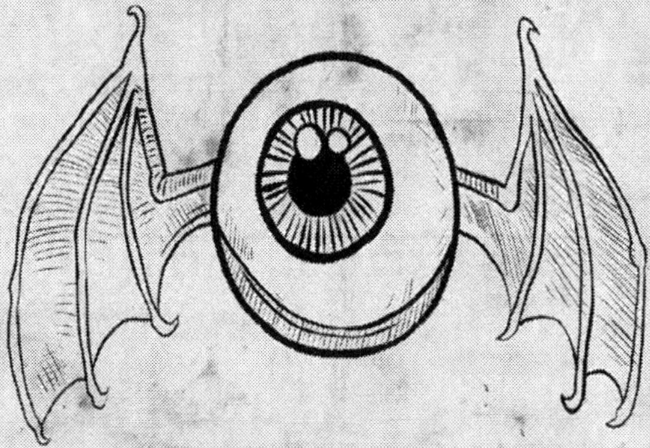

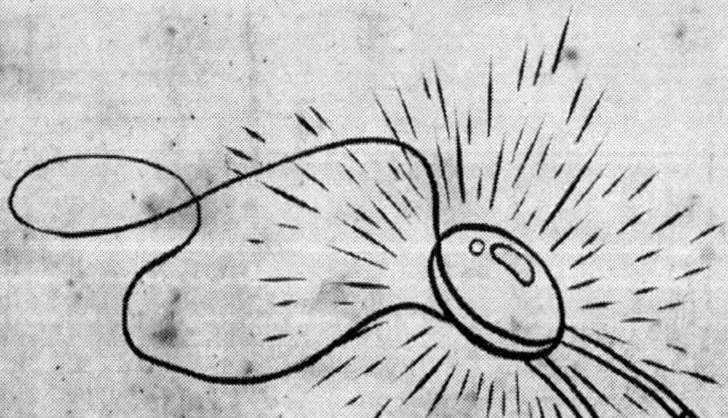

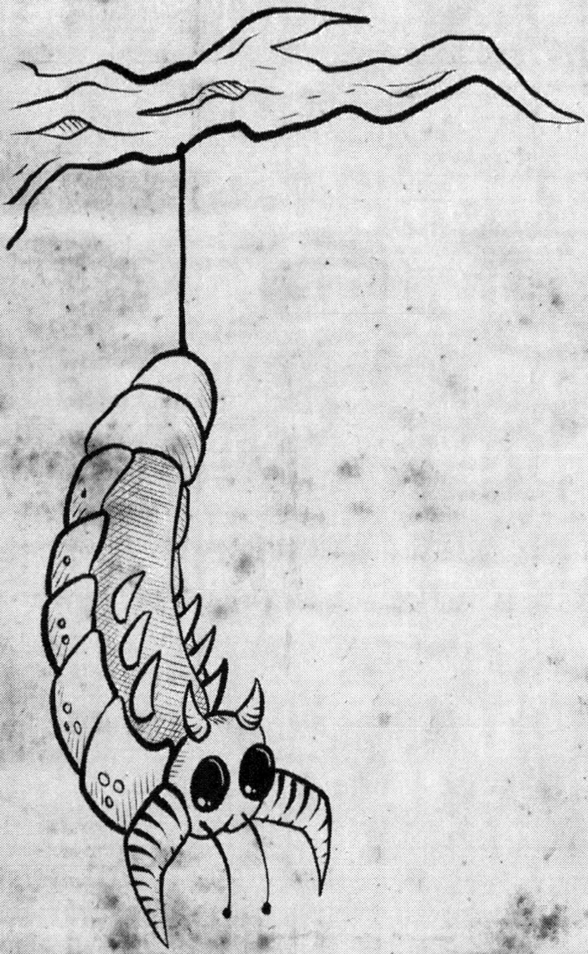

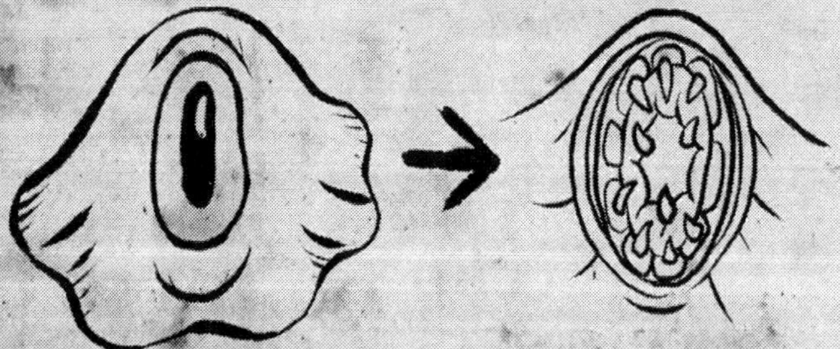

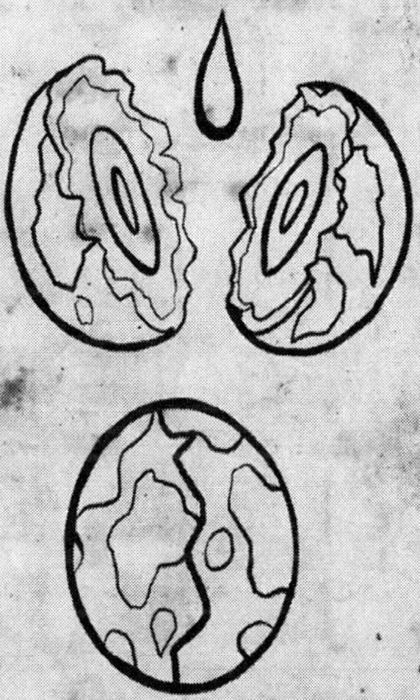

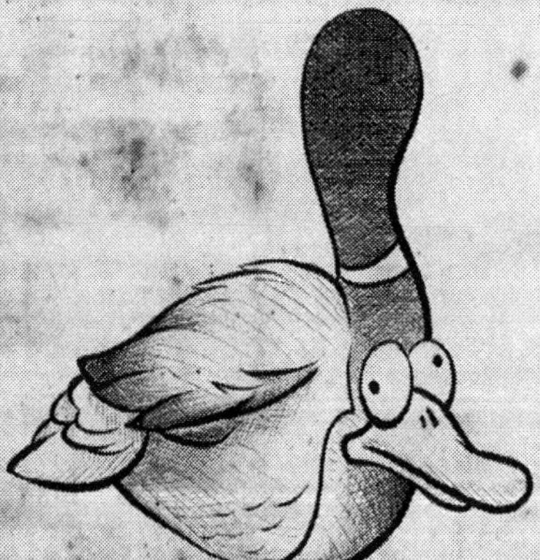

19

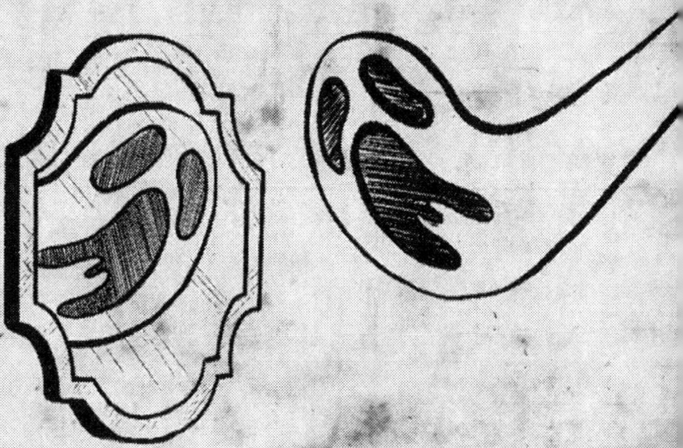

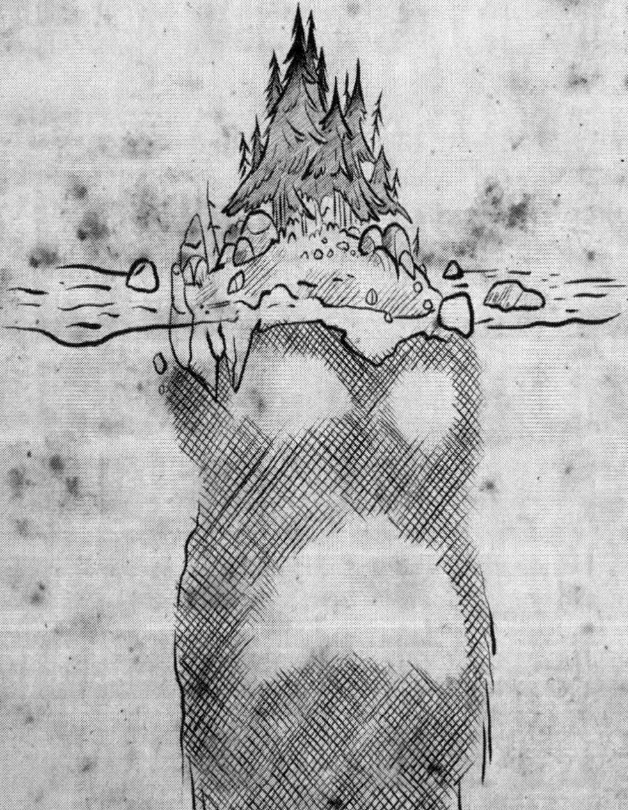

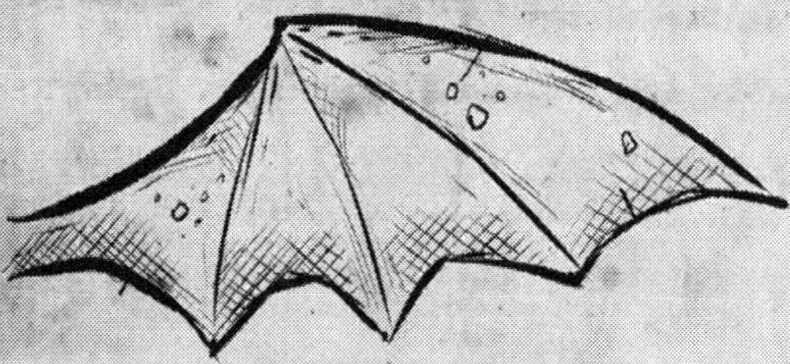

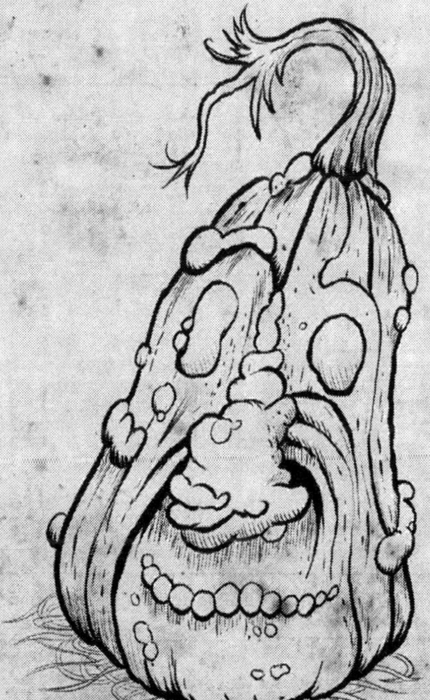

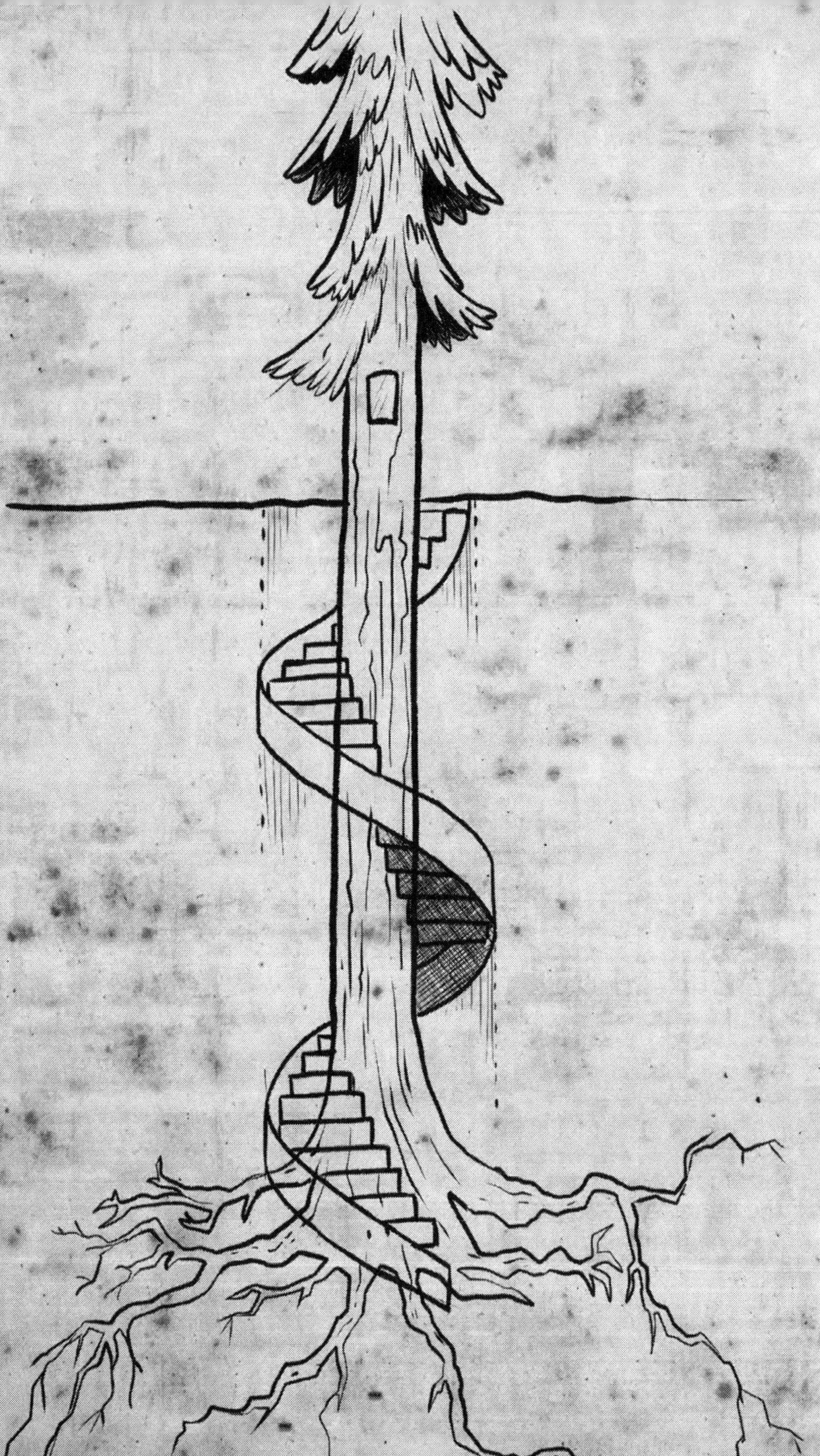

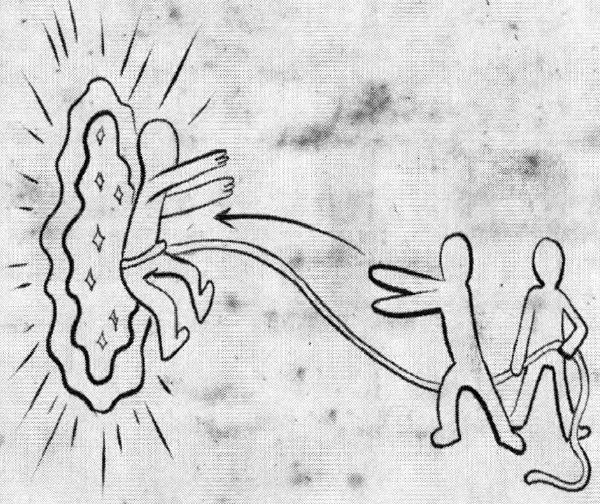

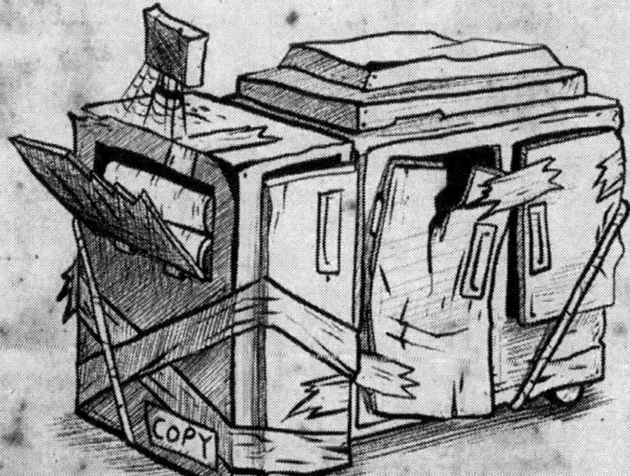
COPY

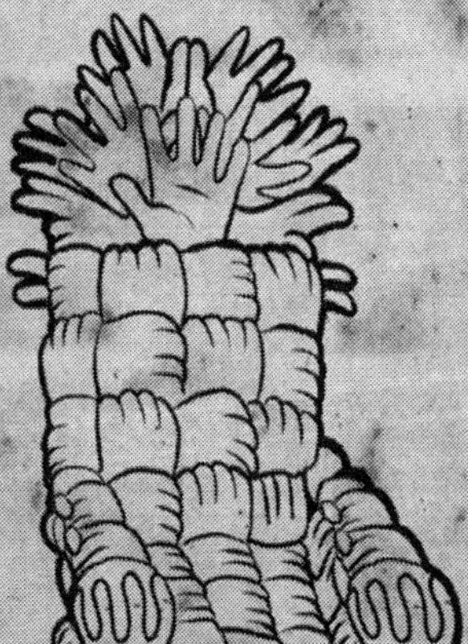

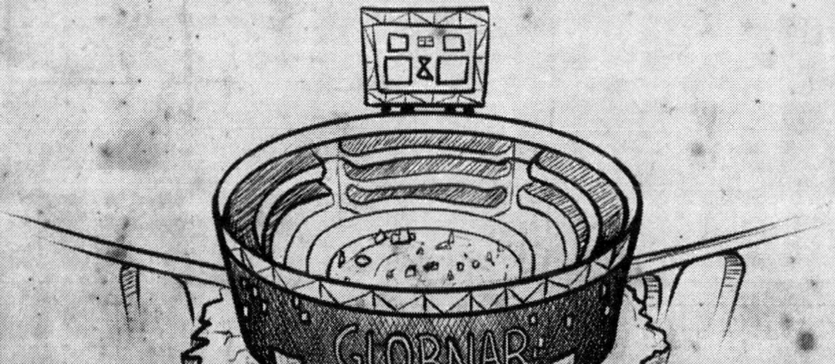
GLOBNAR

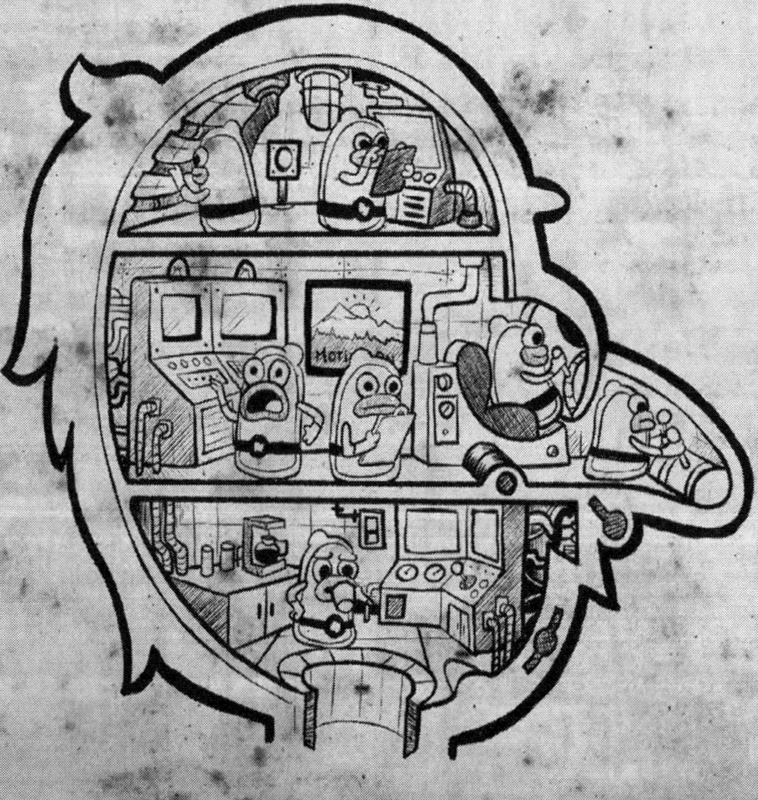

MT

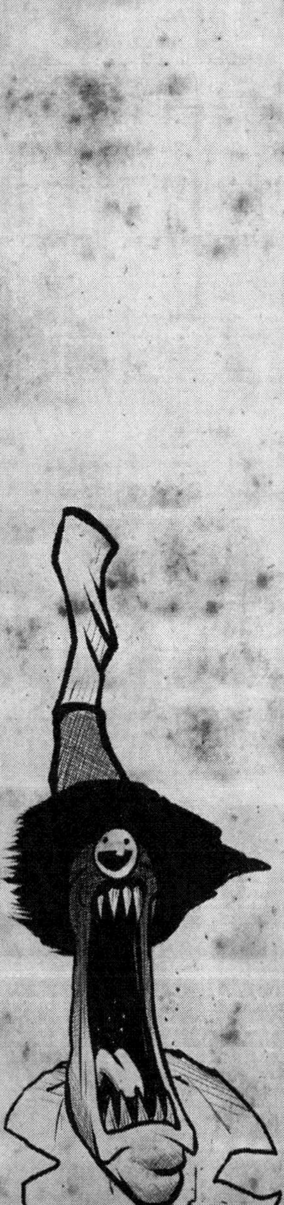

TRUST NO ONE!

Made in the USA
Monee, IL
10 September 2024

0dfc54d5-8001-4228-90a0-c695499b4ce5R01